Successful Mentoring in HR

9 Ways to Turn Your Human Resources Expertise Into Your Own Unique Process for Mentoring Others in HR

Alisa Charles

Successful Mentoring in HR

9 Ways to Turn Your Human Resources Expertise Into Your Own Unique Process for Mentoring Others in HR

Copyright 2017 by Alisa Charles

ISBN-10: 0-9895385-3-2

ISBN-13: 978-0-9895385-3-4

About the Author

Alisa Charles is a certified Senior Professional in Human Resources (SPHR), (SHRM-SCP) with a Bachelor of Arts degree in Communications from the University of Illinois at Chicago, and a Master of Science degree in Human Resources Management and Development from National Lewis University. She also holds a professional coaching certification from the Coaching and Positive Psychology (CaPP) Institute.

Alisa is the creator of HRInventure, which provides creative resources for inventive HR people with adventurous HR careers. She has also worked for several large organizations in various human resources roles for over twenty years. In area, regional, and divisional HR leadership roles, she has had the pleasure of supporting the HR function for multiple locations across the country. This is where her passion for helping HR professionals began.

Alisa is married to Gregoire Charles and has three children; Marcas, Ashley, and Xavier.

Invitation from the Author

Thank you so much for your interest in sharing your HR expertise and knowledge with others. I am thrilled that you may be considering mentoring others in HR as an avenue to accomplish that goal.

This book provides some great ideas and information for Human Resources professionals on how to share your HR expertise by creating an awesome mentoring in HR experience for other HR professionals and students.

It also includes step-by-step strategies on how to build trust, engagement and excitement within the mentoring processing. This is all accomplished by leveraging your own HR expertise, style and talents in your own way.

To help you get started, here is a free tool: Receive 15 complimentary Mentoring in HR templates that will help you create your own unique process for mentoring others in HR faster. Simply use the link below to access. https://hrinventurenetwork.com/get-15-free-templates

Enjoy!
Alisa Charles

Table of Contents

Introduction

Again, thank you for your interest in *Successful Mentoring in HR*. Let me just say that I am very excited that you are reading this book on a topic that has been of interest to me for a very long time.

I feel that it is no accident you are reading this book at this particular moment, especially with so many other priorities you probably have in both your HR world and in life.

However, my guess is, you probably already have some ideas about sharing your HR expertise in some way, and mentoring in HR may be a vehicle that can help you get started.

I am hopeful that after you read this book you will have some additional ideas that will help you to develop a process for mentoring others in HR that fits with your own unique style, approach, and situation.

This book will review a 9-step process that is a flexible one. It is designed simply as a starting point, with some ideas for an HR mentoring process that many of us as

HR professionals usually participate in from time to time over the course of our careers.

While this book will review 9 steps you can use right now to create an awesome HR mentoring experience, you can determine which particular steps are right for you. You can also determine any additional steps you would like to include as part of your own unique process.

The area of HR you are in, will also factor into how you may want to approach mentoring in HR. This book will be a great resource for anyone in any area of HR such as:

- Benefits Administration
- Worker's Compensation and Safety
- Training and Development
- Recruitment
- Employee Relations
- Payroll
- Compensation
- General HR
- HR Associations
- College/University HR programs
- HR Compliance/Legal... and more

If you have found yourself in a situation where you were asked 1) to mentor another HR professional; 2) to mentor a new HR person who has come on board or was recently promoted to an HR role; or 3) to mentor as part of an initiative to work with students in an HR program; then you are in the right place.

In cases where you may have been asked to actually participate in the training process for another HR professional, I would say that training is a different process then mentoring. While training could involve some mentoring, this book will not include any specific HR training resources, tips, or information that can be used to help train other HR professionals.

Instead, this book will focus strictly on mentoring others in HR using 9 steps for an effective and successful mentoring experience. As you read through this book, I want to encourage you to open your mind to all of the amazing possibilities that exist in mentoring others in HR.

For the purpose of this book, I would like to share the following definition for mentoring. *"Mentoring is a process for the informal transmission of knowledge, social capital, and psychosocial support perceived by the recipient as relevant to work, career, or professional development. Mentoring entails information communication, usually face-to-face and during a sustained period of time, between a person who is perceived to have greater relevant knowledge, wisdom, or experience (the mentor) and a person who is perceived to have less (the mentee).[1]*

This definition matches well with successfully mentoring others in HR because it is an opportunity for those who have built their career in HR to share their expertise with others in HR who may be less experienced, such as those early in their career or students.

So whether you currently mentor others, are looking to start an HR mentoring program at work or with an association; or you just want some ideas you can use in the future, this book is a great way to help you get started.

*1. Bozeman, B.; Feeney, M. K. (October 2007). "Toward a useful theory of mentoring: A conceptual analysis and critique". Administration & Society. **39** (6): 719–739. doi:10.1177/0095399707304119*

Message to Readers

I am pleased to share that this is an interactive book. As a result, I want to discuss with you how to bring your reading experience to life.

At the end of each chapter you will have access to a video message from me about that chapter and a brief introduction of the chapter that follows.

You will be able to access the video message via a link or QR (Quick Response) codes that will be provided at the end of each section.

All of the links throughout this book can be used by clicking directly on the link or typing the link address right into your browser.

If you choose to use the QR codes instead, all of the QR codes throughout this book can be scanned with your smartphone or device to watch the videos that were created especially for you.

Each video is less than a minute long. After you have watched the video, I hope you will feel even more inspired and motivated to move forward and create your own process for mentoring others in HR.

The following is additional information on how to scan the QR codes is this book:

Step 1: Download a free QR code reader onto your smartphone or device by searching the App Store.

Step 2: Tap the app once it has downloaded onto your device. Tap again and your camera will appear to come on. Place your device over the code you wish to scan, and the camera will automatically take a picture of the QR code; then your device will be directed to the respective web page on my website on hrinventurenetwork.com to view the video message.

Again, thank for your interest in mentoring in HR.

Alisa Charles

Watch Video Message: Alisa Charles Quick Message to Readers http://hrinventurenetwork.com/quick-message-to-readers/	

1 *My Thoughts on Mentoring in HR*

I remember early in my career when I worked my first HR job in the Student Employment Office while in college. I had applied for a part-time office assistant position and didn't realize the job I applied for was for the actual Student Employment Office. In fact, I used to say that I started in HR by accident. However, looking back on it now, I have come to realize that even though I didn't know it at the time, it was all part of a bigger plan for me in HR.

I ended up working in the Student Employment Office my entire four years of college. I received great exposure to HR in the areas of payroll, recruitment, employee relations, and much more. What I remember most, was the hiring of a person in our department who was always talking about a career in Human Resources. She was very focused on working in HR after her graduation. She also introduced me to the HR associations in our area, and told me about the HR certification process.

Her enthusiasm for HR changed my life. I went from majoring in social work during my first year of college, to sharing how I wanted an HR job after graduation in my senior year. While she was not a formal HR mentor, her influence had such a strong impact on me that it would shape my entire outlook on a career in HR. From there, I did work in several HR positions after graduation and beyond, and it has been a great journey. As a result of that experience, I have always embraced opportunities to help others in HR.

Since you are reading this book, I believe you may have a similar interest in helping other HR professionals as well. This makes me very excited about all of the possibilities you have to create similar experiences for others in Human Resources.

There are several situations where mentoring others in HR would be an amazing way to give back to other HR professionals or students. The following are just a few scenarios where mentoring in HR may be a good solution for you such as:

- You have invested a lot of time and energy building your HR career, and would love the opportunity to share your HR expertise.

- You may have an HR person on your team who is early in their HR career or newly promoted into a new HR role where mentoring could help them to be successful.

- You may belong to a professional HR association that does outreach to students studying HR where mentoring would be beneficial.

- You have always had an interest in helping other HR professionals, and would enjoy being partnered with an HR professional either inside or outside your organization.

- You would like to provide a development opportunity for an existing HR person on your team to mentor others on the team, or participate in peer mentoring of new hires in HR.

- Someone may have reached out to you at a conference, social media, or through a friend or family member, and asked if you would be available to mentor them.

- You are interested in starting a new HR mentoring initiative at a school, association, work, or other organization.

- You would like to be a resource for those who perform HR who are not in your own company, and may not have access to a lot of HR resources, such as a small business or small HR department at another company.

- You are looking for ways to earn HR re-certification credit which can be accomplished by mentoring in HR when certain criteria are met.

Whatever your reasons are for your interest in mentoring, having a system in place will help make the mentoring experience feel less stressful and become a more positive experience for both the HR mentor and mentee.

Watch Video Message: Alisa Charles on Chapter 1 https://hrinventurenetwork.com/Alisa-Charles-chapter1/	

2 *A Few Quick Thoughts for HR Mentors*

One thing to keep in mind from the very beginning about a process like this is, while your HR experience and expertise can make for successful mentoring in HR, mentoring should not be a one-way street. In fact, it should include opportunities to learn from the HR mentee as well.

It is my belief that there should be a good balance between sharing your experiences and learning about the HR mentee's goals, strengths, and how best to work with them to successfully address any challenges. This book will provide several ideas to assist you in achieving this.

The overall goal of mentoring others in HR is to start off with a very friendly and supportive approach. The more prepared you are with a system, the more your HR mentee will have confidence in the process, and you will have greater success in achieving the goals of this HR mentoring partnership.

While there could be many reasons for wanting to mentor others in HR, this book will give you some solid steps to help you develop a process that will be right for you and your situation. Whether you are a part of an HR department, HR association or committee, or looking to do this independently for personal development or HR certification credit (when certain criteria has been met), this resource is for your use, to create the best process for you.

To help you get started with the 9-step process for mentoring others in HR, this next section will discuss how to help you prepare for HR mentoring by exploring your interest a little further.

You will start to think about what your ideal mentee and mentoring process may look like. This will be helpful in developing your own process for your ideal HR mentoring situation.

| **Watch Video Message: Alisa Charles on Chapter 2** https:///hrinventurenetwork.com/alisa-charles-chapter2 | |

3   *Preparing for Mentoring in HR*

Imagine this: Let's say you are at a point where you have actually agreed to mentor another HR professional or HR student. **Now what?**

In this situation, there may be a lot of thoughts that come to mind such as:

- Will I make a good mentor?
- Will I be successful?
- Will I be able to have any impact or make a difference in any way?
- Do I have the time to invest in mentoring someone else?
- What about my other duties and responsibilities?
- How will I fit this all in?

These are all great questions and all very reasonable things to think about. Since the goal is to make this a positive and effective process, I feel it is important to think about these questions now. The reason for this is that it will be difficult to make this process as positive and supportive as possible if you leave these concerns unaddressed.

To help with preparing for successful mentoring in HR, let's explore why you may be interested in mentoring in HR. Once you identify your purpose for wanting to participate in mentoring others, then it will become your foundation and will help you to deal with some of the challenges and questions that may come up along the way, even before you get started.

Let's start with a very basic question. **Why are you interested in mentoring others in HR?**

Take a few minutes to think about this question and your answer. Feel free to go back to the previous section of this book and review the examples listed as to why some HR professionals may have an interest in mentoring in HR.

What did you come up with? What is your answer? Why are you interested in mentoring others in HR?

- To share your HR expertise?
- To make a difference in HR?
- To earn HR certification credit (when certain criteria has been met)?
- To give back?

- To help others in HR?
- To enhance your HR career?
- To follow a passion or aspiration?

There could be many answers to this question, but the most important answer right now is the one that applies to you. I am hopeful you were able to identify one or two good reasons why you are interested in mentoring in HR.

I am also hoping your reason for mentoring someone else in Human Resources isn't because you feel pressured to do so, while having very little interest in doing so at all. If that is the case, I encourage you to either:

1) Find a reason or purpose to move forward with it anyway and participate as an HR mentor in a way that makes you feel more positive or favorable about the opportunity; or

2) Discuss your disinterest as appropriate, and see if you can be removed from being an HR mentor.

If you are not able to feel positive about being an HR mentor, it will show up in some way during the mentoring process. This would not be good for you or the mentee, and could actually do more harm than good for the mentee.

If you feel like mentoring someone is not something that you are really interested in doing, then it's better to not participate in the process in order to avoid a negative experience for the HR professional or student designated to be mentored.

I understand there could be a lot of reasons why mentoring may not be of interest and that is perfectly okay, especially if it is recognized upfront so it doesn't negatively impact anyone else.

I'm going to assume you are reading this book because you are interested in mentoring someone in HR. Therefore, let's focus on your reasons why you would like to mentor in HR. Let's also focus on putting it all together into a process that would work for you.

Some basic things you want to think about as you determine what your process will look like include the following items:

- Do you want to mentor someone inside your company or department, or are you looking to mentor someone outside the organization?

- Should the mentee have an interest in a specific HR area, or is any HR area okay?

- Are you looking to do in-person mentoring, over the phone, online, or a combination?

- Are you interested in developing a mentoring program that would include several mentees or one individual at a time?

- Do you have a preference for mentoring a student in HR or an HR professional?

- Are you looking for a short-term assignment (a few weeks/month), or a longer-term assignment (one year)?

- Do you know how much time you want to spend each week/month on mentoring activities?

Once you determine your ideal HR mentoring parameters, and how long of a commitment you are interested in, you can better develop a process that fits your ideal mentoring situation. For example, if you are only looking to do this over a short period of time, then you may want a less formal approach with fewer tools and resources. However, if you are looking to mentor on a longer-term basis, it is very possible you might be more interested in making this a more formal process, to ensure everything stays on track.

Either way, you want to at least have a general idea how this mentoring partnership will work so that expectations are clear from the very beginning.

Throughout this book, I will be referring to several tools and resources to assist you in creating your own unique process. If you decide you are interested in what these tools could look like, I have already created *Mentoring in HR* templates that you can use to help make developing your own process faster. If you have not already received these complementary templates, at end of this book I share a link to receive them.

Watch Video Message: Alisa Charles on Chapter 3 https://hrinventurenetwork.com/alisa-charles-chapter3	

4 *9 Steps to Mentoring in HR*

Now that you have an idea of why you are interested in being an HR mentor and your ideal HR mentoring setup, let's put it all together with the 9 steps that will help you to quickly start mentoring others in HR.

The 9 steps for successful mentoring in HR are as follows:

1) Create an impactful first impression
2) Build an intriguing foundation
3) Communicate expectations and roles
4) Set goals for HR mentoring success
5) Implement robust HR projects
6) Good follow-up throughout the mentoring partnership
7) Solid wrap up of the mentoring partnership
8) Obtain feedback
9) Follow-up after the mentoring has ended

As we review each step in more detail, you want to think about how you may want to incorporate the suggestions into your own unique process.

Get ready to put your skills, talents, and experience to work by creating a process where all of your efforts and expertise as an HR professional will now benefit others along their HR journey. Are you ready?

Step 1: Create an Impactful First Impression

The first step to successfully mentoring in HR is making a good first impression with impact for your HR mentee. This is a very important part of the process, as it will also set the tone for the entire HR mentoring experience.

Without an impactful presentation from the very beginning, the entire HR mentoring process can end before it even gets started, or soon after, without much benefit at all for the HR mentee.

How you decide to implement this step will be entirely up to you, but I do have some ideas that can help you achieve this. While there are many ways to create an impactful first impression with your HR mentee, here are a few ideas you can consider in the following three areas:

1. Ideas to successfully kick off the HR mentoring

process

2. Ideas to help prepare for the initial meeting with HR mentee

3. Ideas for conducting the initial meeting with HR mentee

Ideas to kick off the HR mentoring process

As a very first step to making an impactful first impression, here are a few ideas you can implement as soon as you become aware of your HR mentee assignment or opportunity.

Any of these ideas are ways you can make a good first impression the moment your HR mentee has been identified.

- Prepare an introductory/welcome communication (letter, email, phone call, recorded audio message, personalized e-card, welcome video)

- Plan an introductory kick off meeting (particularly when there will be a group of HR mentors/mentees involved)

- Provide brochures or resources that you have

from work or other HR resources

- Provide an email with links to HR tools and resources they can immediately use
- Give a small gift or token, such as office or HR products
- A welcome gift basket
- A welcome packet
- Include anything you have personally written or created that will help them get to know you better as a mentor

Again, you can decide which of these ideas you would like to use to kick off this process in an enthusiastic and positive way. You can be as creative and welcoming as you like. Add your own ideas too if you feel they may work better for you.

Just remember that this will be your first interaction in an HR mentor capacity, so you want to make sure that whatever you decide, it delivers the desired outcome of making the HR mentee feel welcomed and motivated about the process.

This exercise also establishes you as the HR expert that you are from the very beginning, by providing HR resources that can assist your mentee even before the mentoring starts. By giving them information, links, gifts, or sharing things you have done in HR already, shows your passion and commitment to the process. It also all adds credibility to you as an HR mentor. This can help create the desired impact needed, resulting in the HR mentee wanting to further engage with you in an HR mentor/mentee capacity.

Once you have completed this first step by creating an impactful first impression, you want to continue on with what you have started, by planning for the first actual meeting with your HR mentee. The following are ideas to help you prepare for the first meeting.

Ideas to prepare for the initial meeting with HR mentee

After implementing a few of the kick off ideas, the next thing you want to do to ensure a good first impression is to start preparing for the initial meeting with your mentee.

Here are a few pre-meeting ideas:

1) Initiate further HR mentor and mentee introductions

2) Inform the HR mentee of tools you will provide to help them prepare for the initial mentoring discussion

3) Inform the HR mentee that you are looking to schedule a date and time with them for the initial mentoring in HR discussion

4) Prepare a sample agenda for them to review prior to the initial meeting

Here is an overview of each one of the four ideas:

Initiate further HR mentor and mentee introductions:
This first (or follow-up) conversation will be an opportunity to welcome the mentee to the mentoring process and to introduce yourself (if you don't already know each other). This could be a brief phone call, video chat, email, or in-person discussion. Its purpose is to share your excitement about working with them, and to let them know that you will be following up with additional information to help prepare them for your first mentoring discussion. This can be a part of your kick off process, conducted at a separate time, or both.

Provide tools to help prepare for the mentoring discussion: Once you complete the introductions, you will then follow-up with items for them to review and/or complete in advance of the first meeting.

I have provided a few suggested tools you can use at this stage. You can decide which items you feel you need, or determine if you have other items you would include as well.

The suggested items include:
- Mentor/mentee job descriptions
- Mentoring in HR partnership agreement
- Mentoring in HR checklist
- Self-assessment tools (questionnaire, application, resume, HR courses completed)

There will be further discussion about these tools in the next section, "Building an Intriguing Foundation" that will provide even more details. Also, toward the end of this book, if you have not received them already, there will be details on how you can access free templates you can use to get started.

Again, you can decide which tools to provide to your HR mentee. After the mentee returns any requested items, you can follow-up with another communication thanking them for getting the information back to you.

Schedule the mentoring in HR meeting: You want to ensure that a date and time is scheduled in advance for the initial meeting with your HR mentee. To accomplish this, you can provide the HR mentee with a few days and times to check their availability. Be sure to request a deadline for their response. Once confirmed, I recommend you send them a written confirmation and a calendar reminder.

Communicate a sample agenda in advance: Finally, before the actual meeting occurs, communicate a draft of the agenda of the items that will be covered during your initial meeting. Along with the agenda, you can include any results from the information that was requested in advance. This will be discussed in further detail in the next section "Building an Intriguing Foundation." If there is any request from either the mentor and/or the mentee to complete items in advance, the results should be shared so the mentee has information about the mentor, and the mentor has information about the mentee as well.

For example, if it was elected that both the mentor and mentee would complete a questionnaire about their background and interests in HR, then the HR mentee should have access to the HR mentor's responses, and the HR mentor should have access to the mentee's responses.

This is a way for both participants to get to know each other a little bit better in advance of the meeting. This will also provide an opportunity for each of them to be prepared with any questions they may have for each other.

Whether there is information to share or not, it is suggested a tentative agenda be communicated in advance, with an opportunity for the HR mentee to request any changes or make any recommendations. Here is a sample of what an agenda may look like:

Sample Agenda

1. Greetings and welcome
2. Expectations and objectives of mentoring partnership
3. Review and discuss questionnaire results

4. Review the Mentoring in HR checklist together and confirm how this process will work

5. Review the Mentoring in HR job descriptions

6. Discuss terms of the HR Mentoring Agreement

7. Confirm goals to be completed by next meeting

8. Other (any other items that need to be discussed)

These pre-meeting ideas can all be wrapped into one process/communication or completed separately, one step at a time. Again, it all depends on your preference and what you feel will work best in your situation.

Now that you have successfully kicked off the process and completed the pre-meeting steps, it is time to continue on with creating a great first impression and conduct the first meeting with your HR Mentee. This first meeting is designed to discuss the expectations of the HR mentoring partnership.

First Meeting to Discuss HR Mentoring Process

We are still talking about making an impactful first impression with your HR mentee. At this point, there has been a welcome/introduction process, information provided to review and complete in advance of this meeting, a sample agenda communicated in advance, and now the time of the scheduled meeting has arrived.

The following are recommendations on how to conduct the first meeting with your HR mentee.

Follow the agenda

The sample agenda was sent out in advance, so by now, any feedback or suggestions about the agenda should have been received and included in an updated agenda. Simply follow the agenda and adjust the conversation as needed.

In the course of following the agenda, you want to also be sure you incorporate certain components into the conversation. As you read these next few suggestions, keep in mind there will be additional information in this book that will help you accomplish them successfully.

Set clear ground rules

As the HR mentor, you want to discuss the ground rules for the HR mentoring partnership. This should include confirming the frequency of meetings, the level of confidentiality, the HR activities that will be included throughout the mentoring partnership, and the exit process.

Confirm the HR mentoring goals and objectives

As part of this initial meeting with your HR mentee, you want to also identify one to three goals to work on as part of the HR mentoring process. The HR mentee would take ownership of the action items and steps; while you as the HR mentor would provide support, feedback, and encouragement. These are goals that should be tracked and updated along the way.

Plan meaningful activities

Work together with the HR mentee to confirm what type of activities would be meaningful to them. For example, if the HR mentee's goal is to obtain more recruitment experience, you could plan for specific recruitment-related activities, such as participating in a mock interview, writing an employment ad, or researching options to post ads to be incorporated in the HR mentoring process.

Incorporate your own creativity and expertise

This process can be as formal or as informal as you like. Keep in mind that mentoring in HR is primarily about building relationships that include mutual trust, confidentiality, and respect. There is also room for you as the HR mentor to incorporate your own style and creativity to add value to the experience.

Adding your own touch is encouraged for a more authentic process that truly reflects each HR mentor's unique style and approach. I hope this adds excitement for you when thinking about how to make this process as much of a reflection of you and your unique style as you choose.

Making an impactful first impression reminders

We have covered quite a bit of information in this area of starting off strong, with a good and impactful first impression. We talked about several different ideas that can be implemented at the start for a very positive and successful HR mentoring partnership. Once the groundwork for a great first impression has been laid, then the rest of the process should be a smooth and organized one.

So let's recap all of those steps you will include in your first impression process:

1) Determine your kick off plan and any giveaways you will provide to your mentee. This could be tools, resources, related links, HR products, or other valuable items or information.

2) Complete the pre-meeting activities prior to the first meeting. This will help ensure an organized first call/meeting. You could also include sending out any tools in advance such as a questionnaire or a request for a resume, confirm a day/time/location for the first meeting, and send a draft of the agenda for review and feedback.

3) Conduct the first meeting with the HR mentee. Start by following the agenda and discuss the expectations of the mentoring partnership. This can be conducted over the phone, in person, online or via videoconferencing.

I am sure there are other ideas you may think of to help create an impactful first impression. Whatever you decide, you want to have your ideas included as part of an actual plan of action at the very beginning. That way you already have a plan or system in place that is ready to be implemented right away.

Think about it this way, let's say YOU are the HR mentee, and an HR professional is going to be working with you to help you develop your HR skills and to help you boost your confidence in the HR field. How impressed would you be if you were welcomed with a nice gift basket and a series of welcome emails showing their excitement and enthusiasm to be working with you? How do you think that would make you feel?

Would you feel differently if you were greeted with phone tag and unable to connect with your mentor right away? Then once the connection is made, it is pretty much limited to "…well if you need anything or have any questions I can answer for you, just let me know." That's it. No plan or expectations that are communicated. No excitement. No next steps. All you receive is a quick phone call and an invitation to ask questions when needed.

That's not a very good first impression. In a case like this, the mentee may be so unmotivated to do much of anything that the mentoring partnership pretty much ends before it even gets started.

That is why the first step of making a good first impression is so vitally important. It generates excitement about the process, shows the mentor's commitment, and lets the HR mentee know that there was some actual thought and planning put into this mentoring partnership.

By putting some focus and effort into making an impactful first impression, you can achieve the desired outcome of making this an engaging process that your HR mentee will be excited about and eager to see where it leads.

In the following section, I am going to discuss the next step, "Building an Intriguing Foundation." This is where we will delve even further into some of the items discussed in the previous section. The tools and resources that will be covered in more detail can add a good level of depth to the HR mentoring process. This is a great approach that will leave your HR mentee feeling intrigued enough that they will want to continue on with the mentoring partnership.

I am hopeful you will see the value in these resources and how they can help your mentoring in HR process become a hugely successful program to your HR mentee.

| **Watch Video Message: Alisa Charles on Chapter 4: Step 1** https:///hrinventurenetwork.com/alisa-charles-chapter4-1 | |

Step 2: Build an Intriguing Foundation

In the first step we talked about some really great reasons for, and ways to create an impactful first impression. Now I want to dig a little deeper into some of the items and tools that were discussed in the last section. The following five tools will assist you in building an intriguing foundation that will help keep your entire HR mentoring process engaging, interesting, and on track.

1. Resume Review
2. Self-Assessment/Questionnaire
3. Job Description
4. HR Mentoring Agreement
5. HR Mentoring Checklist

Before I talk too much about these tools, please be aware that I have created templates for you to use to help you to quickly get started. If you have not already received your complimentary templates, I have a link for you to access them at the end of this book.

This is such an incredible section because through these tools is where the magic in the HR mentoring process happens. As the HR mentor, this is where you find out about your HR mentee, and find ways to impact their life in a way that could last a lifetime. For the HR mentee, this is where they can discover an even greater vision for their HR career, and how you can assist them in achieving even bigger goals then they may have initially aspired to in their career.

This is where the path of the HR mentoring partnership begins to take shape. In my view, whoever has crossed your path to be in a mentoring partnership with you is not there by accident. I strongly believe that once you find yourself in a position to mentor someone else, there is some greater purpose for the connection.

My hope is these tools will help you to discover that purpose and to fulfill it in the way only you can. The purpose may be realized immediately, or sometimes it's simply to plant a seed now that will flourish for your HR mentee later in their career and in life.

There may also be other benefits to the HR mentoring process that may unlock additional aspirations for you. By mentoring in HR, it may expose you to other opportunities, individuals, or situations that can benefit you in ways that may have never occurred otherwise.

In addition to the magic of the HR mentoring process coming to life, these tools will also help you with communicating expectations upfront in a way that will keep your HR mentee interested and engaged in the process. It can also help you to keep things on track, which is critical to keeping the momentum of the process intact.

All of these outcomes together combine to make a foundation in your HR mentoring process that will be sustainable and impactful throughout the entire relationship. With all of these resources working together, it makes it exciting to consider all the possibilities that exist with mentoring others in HR.

The following five tools will help you build an intriguing foundation for the HR mentoring partnership:

1) Resume Review: When looking at a resume for the purpose of getting to know your HR mentee a little better, you will review it differently than when looking at it as you would for a candidate for a position. The purpose of the resume review in a mentoring situation is to learn about your HR mentee, and to determine how you can enhance their HR career goals and aspirations in a meaningful way.

While the resume review is just one way to accomplish this, a task like this will help you get an idea of what they've already done, and where opportunities may exist to expose them to other areas of HR that may be of interest to them.

If your HR mentee is a student and doesn't have a resume, you can ask for their list of HR classes they have taken or will be taking. This way, you can learn about what they have or will be exposed to in the classroom, and plan how you can make it come to life for them with real-world experience and knowledge.

I would also recommend you provide them with your own resume to review as well. This way the HR mentee can get to learn more about you. I encourage you to make it available to them to review in advance of your meeting.

This way, at the time of your initial discussion about the mentoring process, they can come prepared with any questions they may have about things you've already accomplished in HR. Or they may have a particular interest in things you've done that they want to learn more about and/or want to be included in their HR mentoring process with you.

This creates a good foundation for building rapport and getting to know each other even before that first meeting occurs. This is important because it will make it more comfortable at the start of this process when there has been this exchange of information to help both parties learn about each other.

2) Self-Assessment/Questionnaire: To continue the process of building a strong foundation, it is recommended you provide your mentee with some form of a questionnaire or assessment to better gauge what they are looking for in the mentoring in HR process.

This assessment could be as simple as a few questions where you ask them about their HR career and/or about HR goals they hope to accomplish through this mentoring partnership. It will also be an opportunity for you to complete information about yourself and your background. This allows for a process that is a shared experience where you're sharing a little bit about yourself and they're sharing a bit about themselves.

Some simple questions that might be included in such an assessment could be questions that really help the participants learn about each other. For example, questions the HR mentor answers could include: What is my interest in being an HR mentor? What HR experiences can I share? What is my background in HR?

Some questions the HR mentee could answer could include: What are my HR goals and aspirations? What areas of HR do I have the most interest in? What is my time frame for accomplishing my HR goals?

This self-assessment can be in the form of a link to an electronic survey, questions included in an email for them to respond to, or any other method you prefer. Whatever the form, it should be a flexible tool that helps to ensure the HR mentoring arrangement is one that meets the goal and objectives of the HR mentee.

3) Job Description: The next recommended tool is a brief job description for the HR mentor and the mentee. This can include basic information that helps to clarify expectations for both the mentor and the mentee. The more tools you have as part of your process that confirm exactly what the process is and is not will be very helpful. It's a way to ensure the expectations are clear from the beginning. It also reduces the chance of disappointment in the process due to a miscommunication of the scope or intentions of the mentoring partnership.

When it comes to a job description, you want something that helps to generally clarify what the HR mentoring partnership will deliver throughout the mentoring experience. To get started, develop a purpose for each position to include at the beginning of the job description. Then list the duties, expectations, and requirements each would be responsible for meeting.

This tool, like all the other recommended tools and resources, are optional. But if you decide to incorporate any of them into your process, please feel free to develop and/or revise in the way you feel will work best for you and your particular program.

The following is some sample language you can use to incorporate into a job description or expectations for both the HR mentor and HR mentee.

HR Mentor

Purpose: To provide advice and guidance to individuals looking to enhance their HR career for greater career development in HR.

Duties and Responsibilities:

- Develop a clear understanding of expectations of the mentoring relationship
- Establish a positive mentoring relationship that includes trust and confidentiality

- Offer encouragement and create an environment of respect
- Initiate an assessment process

HR Mentee

Purpose: To receive guidance and support for greater career development in HR.

- Have a clear understanding of your expectations for your HR mentor
- Clearly communicate those expectations
- Listen and contribute to the conversation
- Follow through on goals and tasks in a timely manner

4) HR Mentoring Agreement: Another tool that can help with building an intriguing foundation is developing a mentoring agreement between you and your HR mentee. This is a great way to set the foundation of the mentoring partnership by putting in writing exactly what the partnership will include from the beginning to the end.

The agreement would include items such as the effective date and the end date of the agreement, details regarding the frequency and type of interaction such as in person, over the phone, online videoconferencing, and/or email.

It could also include expectations about canceling or changing meetings, and any other details that would be beneficial to include in the agreement.

You can also add any specifics about goals, projects, or other items to be accomplished during the mentoring process. The agreement can be as long or as short as you would like. It can also include as much detail or as few details as you feel is appropriate. It's a great tool to have that will help to confirm what the expectations will be with regard to the arrangement.

The following is a sample of what this agreement could look like:

1. Our HR Mentoring Agreement will begin on (date) and end on (date) as follows:

2. We will meet (weekly/monthly) at (time) for (thirty minutes, one hour).

3. We will meet (list location, phone, video conference, or conference call).

4. The objectives of the HR mentoring experience will include:
   - List item
   - List item
   - List Item

5. The knowledge, skills, and experience that will be shared includes:

HR Mentor Signature/Date_____

HR Mentee Signature/Date_____

The example shared above shows just a few items that could be included in your mentoring agreement. You can add, change, or revise any of the items in your agreement as you choose. This is an optional tool that is very flexible and can be customized for your specific needs and based upon your own style and preferences.

5) HR Mentoring Checklist:

One last item that can be an effective tool is a one-page overview of all the steps included in this process in the form of a checklist. This checklist would clearly outline the steps you would want included as part of your own unique process for mentoring others in HR.

You could include all your pre-planning activities that occur prior to the first meeting with your HR mentee, as well as all the activities that will occur during and after the initial discussion. Including all of the follow-up steps that will occur throughout the process will help you to stay organized and on track.

If you will be meeting with your HR mentee monthly, weekly, or quarterly, that schedule should also be included in the checklist. You can also add the dates and times of meetings, goal deadlines, progress updates, and any additional activities that will occur at the end of the mentoring partnership and beyond.

Having all of this information as part of checklist will help to keep the process moving along at a good pace. As discussed earlier, the last thing you want is a process that loses its steam after a while due to lack of follow-up, or no clarity on how follow-up communication will occur. This tool will help keep the process moving along by helping you monitor the steps and keep things moving along according to schedule.

The following are a few examples of steps that could be included in the checklist:

HR Mentor:

- Have HR mentee complete a self-assessment
- Complete an HR mentor self-assessment
- Share each others' assessments results to start foundation of mentoring relationship
- Establish confidentiality

HR Mentee:

- Openly share experiences, goals, and objectives
- Determine which HR competencies need improvement
- Determine future growth and development opportunities in HR
- Gain a better understanding of best practices in HR

Watch Video Message: Alisa Charles on Chapter 4: Step 2 https:///hrinventurenetwork.com/alisa-charles-chapter4-2	

Step 3: Communicate Expectations and Roles

This next section is Step 3 of the 9-step process for successful mentoring in HR, which covers communicating expectations and roles. While many of the key components of this section have already been discussed in the prior two sections, I want to reiterate how important this step is to the overall success of your HR mentoring process.

This is another key section, because neither the HR mentor nor the mentee should ever feel like they are entering into a process that is uncertain or undefined. By discussing, or confirming in writing all of the components of the HR mentoring partnership at the very beginning, it ensures everyone is on the same page and knows what to expect as the process moves forward.

For example, it could be that the HR mentee might be expecting something different from this mentoring partnership, such as assistance with a job search, or the delegation of actual HR work assignments to the HR mentor. They may not be fully aware of the true purpose of the HR mentoring process, which is about helping them realize their potential by developing their confidence and skills with encouragement, support, and communication from an HR mentor along the way.

Or an HR mentor may feel that this is a process with no structure or goals and is just a random partnership that can cut into their time at any random moment. This can cause a feeling of lack of control over their own schedule and availability to mentor, which in turn could cause stress about the process, and even make one think differently about being an HR mentor.

Both perceptions can be corrected if discussions about the process are handled at the very beginning by confirming the scope, goals, meeting times, and end date of the HR mentoring partnership. This is not to say that a mentoring relationship couldn't develop into a connection or a future HR opportunity. It is also possible that the mentoring partnership could assist in some way with actual HR projects. This will be discussed later in this book. But generally speaking, that would not be the initial purpose of mentoring in HR.

Some of the tools and resources that were mentioned in Step 2 can certainly help with you this. In fact, there are three in particular that are available to help you communicate roles and expectations:

1. Job Description
2. HR Mentoring Agreement
3. HR Mentoring Checklist

In addition to those tools, good communication can help to prevent any confusion about the process. Here are some examples of clarifying questions that could be asked:

- What other expectations do you have regarding this HR mentoring partnership?
- Are there any other items you would like to include as part of this HR mentoring partnership arrangement?
- Do you have any further questions about this process?

- What do you hope to accomplish by the end of the HR mentoring partnership?

- Are there any other questions, comments, or concerns you may have about this process?

There are also several strategies to assist you with good communication, and reinforcing the roles and expectations of the HR mentor and HR mentee, such as the following:

Ongoing Communication: After the initial communication has been completed, then any ongoing communication you can do along the way is recommended.

Further communication can be in the form of written or verbal confirmations, such as a follow-up phone call, in-person conversations, text messages, emails, cards, letters, or any other method you choose. For example, you may want to send confirmations along the way confirming meeting dates, projects, goals, to reiterate your role as their HR mentor, and/or your expectations of them as the HR mentee.

Respectful Communication: Whatever way you choose to communicate with your HR mentee regarding roles or expectations, you want to remember to keep the communication as clear and concise as possible. You also want to make sure that communication is respectful and professional at all times.

For example, if your HR mentee is running late for a call, a meeting, or achieving a goal, you do not want that situation to go unaddressed. By doing so, then one late call can turn into not showing up at all for the next call. Then the next thing you notice is that there is no further communication, and the process begins to dissolve before you know it.

A simple communication reminding them of the expectation, whatever it may be, in a supportive and positive way, is a great way to help keep things on track. This also helps to keep the HR mentoring partnership free from judgment or negativity. This gentle reminder, in most cases, is all that would be needed to keep the HR mentoring process moving along as planned.

Active Listening: Finally, you want to ensure you engage in active listening. This will allow you to recognize both verbal and nonverbal cues from your HR mentee and decide whether further explanation or clarification may be needed. It can also help to confirm understanding and agreement of the roles and expectations of the HR mentoring partnership, and that everyone is in agreement with the plan.

I am thrilled about all the ways you can keep the communication of roles and expectations flowing throughout the HR mentoring process. As the HR mentor, your energy and follow through will be important to keeping the process alive, the momentum high, and in helping the HR mentee to stay motivated and engaged in the process.

Now that we have established ways to ensure roles and expectations are clearly communicated, the next step in the 9-step process is about setting goals for mentoring in HR success.

| Watch Video Message: Alisa Charles on Chapter 4: Step 3 https:///hrinventurenetwork.com/alisa-charles-chapter4-3 |  |

Steps 4: Set Goals for HR Mentoring Success

Setting clear goals is another key to a successful

mentoring in HR process. It is important that the goals are set right at the beginning of the partnership for the best results. The goals I am talking about here are not the same as the HR projects I will be discussing in the next step.

For the purpose of successful mentoring in HR, there are three types of goals I want to recommend as part of your process. Again, you can decide which goals you want to include, or other types of goals you may want to add as part of your own unique plan.

Once these goals have been determined during discussions with the HR mentee, you can choose to include them in the HR Mentoring Agreement. Here are three areas where setting goals can bring even greater clarity to the process.

- Meeting goals – These are goals you can set related to the frequency of meetings. It may be determined that you both want to meet five times throughout the process. You can both decide if these meetings would be every week, bi-weekly, every month, or every quarter. You can also decide how these meetings will be conducted such as in person, via phone, videoconferencing, or some other way.

Once these details are established, you might add the following to your agreement:

During the HR mentoring partnership the HR mentor/mentee agree to meet five times, to consist of every other week for the next ten weeks. The first and last meeting will be in-person meetings, and the remaining three meetings will be conducted via videoconferencing.

- HR goals – Once you have more information about the interests of your HR mentee and how you can assist them in their HR journey, you can suggest areas in HR to be incorporated into the HR mentoring partnership. For example, if the HR mentee wants to learn more about recruitment, employee relations, or benefits administration, you can set these areas as general HR goals to be covered in the mentoring process.

Perhaps there are certain HR competencies that they would like to know more about. Those specific competencies can be identified and an HR goal established around them so that they are included in the HR mentoring process. An HR goal may look something like the following:

During the Mentoring in HR partnership, the HR mentor/mentee agree to cover areas on the topic of employee relations by sharing knowledge, experience, and best practices. Furthermore, at least one HR project will be focused on employee relations.

- HR activity goals - Once it has been determined how often you will meet with your HR mentee and you learn the areas of HR that are of interest to your HR mentee, you can now begin to start setting goals about the type of HR activities that will be included in the HR mentoring partnership.

The types of activities that can be included are limitless. Here is where you can get those big ideas flowing and really get creative.

Some examples of HR activities could include such things as:

1) Arrange to meet with an HR executive, Benefits Director, or any HR person in your HR world who could add value to your HR mentee's experience.

2) Have them join in on at least one conference call, HR meeting, or training you conduct.

3) Have them conduct research on an HR topic of their interest and write a proposal on an idea that the HR mentee will present at their own HR job or class.

Once these goals have been determined, I recommend you develop a way keep track of the status of each goal. For example, you may want to list three or four goals that have been agreed upon, where both the HR mentor/mentee will periodically update the progress and status of each goal.

The overall objective would be that all the goals are achieved by the end of the mentoring partnership. Also, the objective includes ensuring that the HR mentee feels like they participated in a valuable exercise that will help them in the next phases of their HR career.

In the next step, we are going to put these goals into action by developing specific HR projects based upon the goals that were set in this step. Here is where the ideas will turn into exciting and robust projects that will keep your HR mentee motivated and excited about their HR mentoring partnership with you.

| **Watch Video Message: Alisa Charles on Chapter 4: Step 4** https:///hrinventurenetwork.com/alisa-charles-chapter4-4 | |

Step 5: Implement Robust HR Projects

Here is another exciting part of the Mentoring in HR process. In this step, we will discuss how to take all of the ideas from the goals that were established and developed with your HR mentee and turn them into specific HR projects that will meet those goals.

This step should evolve into HR projects that will enhance your HR mentee's experience, and to keep moving the mentoring partnership process along in a positive, fun, and exciting way.

What makes this step a little easier is that a lot of the work has already been completed. At this point in the process, you would already know the HR mentee's interests, and what goals have been determined. You will have everything you need to determine the specific HR projects that will be accomplished throughout the HR mentoring partnership.

I recommend the HR projects that are identified, are projects where the HR mentee would actually have to perform a specific task or action. For example, if the HR mentee is interested in the area of recruitment, then the HR project should include a specific task or action related to recruitment.

This could include such tasks as:

1) Outline a recruitment strategy for a specific open position.
2) Develop creative advertising for internal and external use to help promote an open position.
3) Take a free course to improve interviewing skills.
4) Suggest a proposal to change or enhance the current recruitment process.

Whatever HR project is established, make sure the project includes actionable steps that will add value to your HR mentee's own experience and HR journey.

Make sure each HR project is specific and includes action steps, resources needed, timeframes, and deadlines. The more detail that can be outlined at the beginning offers for less chance for any miscommunication about the project, goal, and outcome.

When it comes to determining the HR projects, there should be a good balance between a project that is challenging and one that is engaging. You certainly don't want to set your HR mentee up with a project that is overwhelming or nearly impossible to complete. Instead, it should provide the opportunity to successfully learn something new that will add to their overall HR experience.

The right type of HR project can have a strong impact on their overall view of HR. In fact, I remember one specific project that really made a difference for me early in my career, when I was working in the Student Employment Office. We were trying to promote the employment services on campus. I volunteered to help to create an advertisement that would go on the shuttle buses which had routes that picked up and dropped off students throughout the campus, all day, every day.

I designed a draft of what the ad could look like. When the draft was turned into a professionally designed advertisement that was placed on all the university shuttle buses, I was amazed to see my idea come to life. I was very proud of that project, and it made me feel that I contributed in a way that made a difference. It also helped with getting more students to use the available services in the employment office, which was the goal.

This particular experience is where my motivation to share my ideas in HR began. From that point on, I was always very eager to share my ideas or try something new in HR. That has been very consistent with each HR position I have had, even up to now with writing this book *Successful Mentoring in HR.* If there are HR projects you have worked on that have inspired you in some way, then you may want to consider incorporating those experiences into your own HR mentoring process.

At this point, all of the details of the mentoring partnership have been discussed, confirmed, and put into action with your HR mentee. Now it's time to talk about how to keep up the momentum with a solid plan for follow-up.

Watch Video Message: Alisa Charles on Chapter 4: Step 5 https:///hrinventurenetwork.com/alisa-charles-chapter4-5	

Step 6: Good Follow-Up Throughout the Mentoring Partnership

We are at Step 6 of the 9-step process to successful mentoring in HR. We have talked about starting off with a good first impression and discussed several tools such as job descriptions, mentoring agreement, checklists, assessments, and more.

We've also talked about HR goals and projects, which will be the main components of the successful mentoring in HR experience. You may have decided to implement one HR project, or maybe three or more as part of your HR mentoring plan. Whatever the case, all of the details should be outlined in a way where you can track the progress and determine if goals and objectives are being met.

This step is important to keep everything on track with consistent and purposeful follow-up throughout the entire HR mentoring partnership.

At the beginning of this process, you may have already determined if the follow-up meetings would be once a month, once a week, or once a quarter. Whatever has been agreed upon, you want to ensure they occur as stated, as this will be critical to the entire success of the HR mentoring process.

If these will be in-person meetings, you want to make sure there is a place reserved where conversations can occur with a minimum of distractions. If this will be a follow-up meeting that will occur over the phone, online or with videoconferencing, ensure that details on how to access the meeting have been provided in advance.

I want to reiterate that the meeting time should not be time that is rushed, or where there is multitasking happening. This time should be dedicated just for this process where both parties have the ability to be fully engaged and enjoy good conversation about the process.

In addition to getting an update on how things are going and how the HR projects are moving along, this is also an opportunity to make sure this is still an effective process for your HR mentee. These follow-up conversations will assist you in determining if the HR mentee is still feeling the value of this experience, and to determine if any adjustments need to be made.

To accomplish these tasks, I recommend an approach similar to that of the very first meeting. You want to be sure you have an agenda determined in advance of each follow-up meeting. Start off by checking in with how things are going, how things are at work or school since your last discussion, ask about any updates on their HR projects, and finally, what they need from you to accomplish the next goal or task.

This follow-up discussion is also a way of making sure the communication is flowing both ways. You want to make sure that as the HR mentor, the conversation is not one-sided where you find yourself doing most of the talking. Instead, you want to ensure the HR mentee is given plenty of opportunity to share their thoughts, updates, or anything else they may want to express about the HR mentoring experience at that point.

These follow-up meetings can take anywhere from thirty minutes to an hour, or even more depending on the timeframe you and your HR mentee have agreed upon in advance. The frequency of meetings may help determine how long each meeting should be. For example, if this is a process where meetings occur on a quarterly basis, you may want to plan on more time to meet. However, if this is a process where you and your HR mentee are meeting on a more frequent basis, such as weekly, bi-weekly, or monthly, then less time may be required for these follow-up discussions.

After several follow-up meetings have occurred, you can conduct additional follow-up activities in between the scheduled meetings, to ensure everything continues to move along smoothly. This additional follow-up can be conducted via email, text message, or even a quick phone call or video chat.

The following are sample communication questions you can use at any time throughout the HR mentoring process:

1) How is your week going so far?
2) What where some of your recent successes?
3) What challenges did you have that I can assist you with?

By utilizing some of these questions, you are able to obtain good information from the HR mentee about how they're doing, what's working well, and what may not be meeting their expectations. This is important because it will allow you to adjust the process if needed.

In the next step, we will discuss ways to wrap up the successful mentoring in HR process. I will discuss ideas that pull together all the great work and effort that will make both the HR mentor and mentee feel proud of all that has been accomplished.

Watch Video Message: Alisa Charles on Chapter 4: Step 6 https:///hrinventurenetwork.com/alisa-charles-chapter4-6	

Step 7: Solid Wrap Up of the Mentoring Partnership

Successful mentoring in HR involves an investment from both the HR mentor and mentee. As a result, when it is time to end the HR mentoring partnership, it should be done in a way where both individuals feel recognized and appreciated for all the contributions and efforts made during the HR mentoring partnership.

For example, can you imagine partnering with an individual who was there to help you grow and develop in HR for a period of time? Imagine there being a lot of success experienced by completing HR projects or accomplishing other HR goals, but when it's all over, there is a cold or awkward ending, as if none of these experiences occurred at all.

I recommend a wrap up process where neither participant feels like there was an abrupt end to the process, with no proper closure. A process where there is a positive ending of the HR mentoring partnership, filled with recognition and appreciation by all parties is best.

An approach that can assist with this would be to set aside time to have a wrap up conversation about the HR mentoring experience. This could occur as part of the last follow-up discussion, where a final status of HR goals and projects are discussed. You can confirm what was achieved, what tasks they will carry on beyond the HR mentoring partnership, and what feedback they may have about the process.

Most importantly, this should be a time to celebrate all that has been accomplished during the entire process. Your high energy, praise, and acknowledgment toward your HR mentee about all that they have achieved is critical. You want this HR mentoring experience that you have created for them to end with great impact.

Just like in the beginning where we talked about all the ways to make a good first impression, you want to take a similar approach when it comes to closing out the process with your HR mentee. Review the list of ideas that were recommended in the first step to help determine ideas to incorporate into this step.

Other ways to close out the process could include a certificate of completion you create or a letter of recommendation, card, or email, your write.

Your HR mentee may be able to use these for special credit in school, or can be shared with their supervisor to show everything that was accomplished during the HR mentoring partnership. Throwing a small party, lunch, dinner, or giving a small gift can all offer a lasting final impression of the mentoring in HR experience too. You may also want to discuss any ideas or expectations they may have about what will occur after the HR mentoring process has ended.

To further assist you with this step, I have provided a sample wrap-up checklist that will help get you started with creating a process that works for you:

Sample Checklist

1) Have a final review of the HR mentoring process that includes the progress of goals and objectives

2) Provide opportunity to share feedback on the process such as:

- What was most effective with this process?
- How will this experience be applied going forward?
- What worked well and what were some opportunities for improvement?
- What areas will you continue to develop?

3) End with positivity and gratitude for all that was accomplished

4) Take the time to celebrate the successes

5) Confirm if there will be any post-mentoring communication/activity

In the next step, I will be talking more about getting feedback about the successful mentoring in HR process. In addition to discussing feedback during the final conversations, the next step will share more ways to get the information that will help you continue to enhance your HR mentoring process for the future.

| **Watch Video Message: Alisa Charles on Chapte 4: Step 7** https:///hrinventurenetwork.com/alisa-charles-chapter4-7 | |

Step 8: Obtain Feedback

As you continue to reflect on the successful mentoring in HR process, it will be important to know what worked well, and what areas you would like to change or improve. This is especially helpful if you are looking to repeat this process with other HR mentees in the future.

Even after the mentoring in HR process has ended, there are a variety of ways to get this feedback. I will discuss two approaches that are quick and easy to implement.

The first approach is to simply ask for the feedback. You can do this with just a conversation over the phone, online, or via email. It should include questions for recommendations regarding improvements or any other thoughts the mentee may have.

You can also try another approach, which is to utilize an online survey to get feedback on your mentoring in HR process. This is a great method whether you have one HR mentee or several HR mentees participating in your program. You simply create the survey with a few questions and send it to all your participants to complete.

This is a great way to get the feedback you are looking for to continue to enhance your process. The following are just a few examples of questions you may want to ask as part of your feedback process.

Since the HR Mentoring Experience…

- How do you feel about your HR career?
- How have your HR skills been improved?
- How confident do you feel in your HR role?
- What do you feel were the highlights?
- Describe the overall quality of the experience.
- What would you have liked to see as part of this experience that was not included?
- What suggestions do you have?

Obtaining responses to these questions will offer you good information that will help you enhance your program. This will allow you to ensure an HR mentoring process that will positively impact the HR careers of others.

We are now approaching Step 9 of the 9-step process for successful mentoring in HR. We have covered a lot of information up to this point such as creating a good first impression, robust HR projects, good follow-up, a positive end to the HR mentoring process, and obtaining feedback.

The last step will discuss a few recommendations for additional follow-up ideas with your HR mentee once the process has ended.

<table>
<tr><td>Watch Video Message: Alisa Charles on Chapter 4: Step 8
https:///hrinventurenetwork.com/alisa-charles-chapter4-8</td><td></td></tr>
</table>

Step 9: Follow-up After the Mentoring Has Ended

Prior to the HR mentoring partnership ending, you and your HR mentee can determine what post-mentoring activities will occur. You can also determine the timing of such follow-up such as thirty, sixty, or ninety days after the HR mentoring partnership has been completed.

By determining these actions with your HR mentee in advance, you will know exactly what they are interested in as far as follow-up. These will be great opportunities to continue to check in with them and see how things are going, even beyond the HR mentoring partnership.

This post-mentoring follow-up can be an informal phone call, email, or whatever way you and your HR mentee agree upon. This step is a great way to reinforce the experience that occurred with the HR mentee during the HR mentoring experience, and to see how some of the things they wanted to continue with after the mentoring process are coming along.

It is also a great opportunity to continue with the connection, to keep the door open for any assistance you can provide in the future, and to reinforce the value of the investment that was made by both HR mentor and HR mentee.

To further assist with this idea, the following is sample language that could be included in a post-mentoring follow-up discussion or email:

Sample Language for Follow-up:

Hello "HR Mentee Name,"

I hope you are doing well. It's been several (weeks, months) since our HR mentor partnership ended. As we discussed during our last conversation, I want to follow-up with you to see how things are going.

When we last talked, you were interested in continuing to develop in the following areas:
• List item
• List item
• List item

I would love to know how your progress has been going.

I am hopeful that you are making the level of progress you desire.

I would also like to know if there have been any other updates since our last conversation.

Of course, whatever follow-up activities are decided is completely up to you and your HR mentee. Other ways to follow-up could be to meet up for coffee or a meal, attend an HR conference or training together, or schedule a series of follow-up calls or videoconferences.

This brings us to the end of the 9 steps to successful mentoring in HR. By incorporating each of these 9 steps, you are ready to create an amazing experience in the way that only **you** can deliver. What is so great about each step, is that you make all the decisions about which suggestions you want to include in your own unique process.

Feel free to re-read each of the 9 steps as many times as you would like as you develop your own system.

| Watch Video Message: Alisa Charles on Chapter 4: Step 9
https://hrinventurenetwork.com/alisa-charles-chapter4-9/ | |

5 | *Successful Mentoring in HR Examples*

Now that you are familiar with the 9 steps for successful mentoring in HR, the following are some examples of how you can put these steps into action.

As mentioned throughout this book, these steps are intended to provide the basics of what you may want to include in a mentoring program for human resources professionals and/or students. Again, you can decide which pieces make sense for your process, or how formal or informal of a process you would like.

You are always welcome to customize a process that works within your schedule, interests, and with your ideal mentee in mind.

Example 1: The Early Career HR Professional

HR Mentee: an HR professional in an entry-level HR generalist position

HR Mentor: a senior HR professional who works in same department and has volunteered to spend some time with this HR professional in a very informal HR mentoring partnership

Purpose for HR Mentoring:

In this example, the HR mentee has worked in HR briefly and is looking for mentoring to help build confidence in their role. The HR mentee is interested in pursuing a graduate degree in Human Resources. They are not sure yet which direction in HR they will pursue, but feel that working with an HR mentor will help them get better clarity regarding their HR career direction.

Step 1: Create an impactful first impression

- HR mentor will start creating a great first impression right away by inviting HR mentee to meet in a conference room at the office where they both work. They will have a very brief discussion about the HR mentoring partnership at a day and time that works for both of them.

- During this discussion, the HR mentor will take the opportunity to share enthusiasm for working with the HR mentee, explain what to expect regarding the process, and explain that an introductory email will be forthcoming which will provide some next steps.

- Also during this discussion, the HR mentor will continue making an impactful first impression by presenting the HR mentee with a small gift to help kick off the process. It is a mug engraved with a funny motivational HR quote.

- After the discussion, the HR mentor will send the introductory email that includes a few HR links to resources the HR mentee can use right away. Also included in the email is a request to send a copy of their resume, and to provide a day and time available for the follow-up meeting about the mentoring in HR partnership.

- HR mentor will continue to follow-up with a thank-you email for receiving the resume. The HR mentor will also send a sample agenda for review and feedback from the HR mentee, a confirmation of the meeting time, and copy of their own resume to be reviewed by the HR mentee.

- During the follow-up meeting, both the HR mentor and mentee will discuss HR interests, desired frequency of meetings going forward, and

HR goals and projects. This will all be finalized in an HR Mentoring Agreement.

Step 2: Build an intriguing foundation

- The tools used for building an intriguing foundation for this partnership will be the resume reviews and the HR Mentoring Agreement.

Step 3: Communicate expectations and roles

- The tools used for communicating expectations for this partnership will be the HR Mentoring Agreement and ongoing follow-up.

Step 4: Set goals for HR mentoring success

- Meeting Goal: To meet five times over the next ten weeks, every two weeks

- HR Goal: To feel more confident in current role. To become more familiar with careers in HR. To identify specific HR areas in current job to become more familiar with.

- HR Activity Goal: Research different careers in HR and discuss findings. Find a training or online course in a specific area. Gain exposure to other areas of HR.

Step 5: Implement robust HR projects

- The HR mentee will sign up and complete online training in a task that is part of their current job, but which they lack confidence: leave of absence administration.

- The HR mentee will rotate a half-day each in three other HR areas (payroll, benefits and recruitment), including sitting in on a staff meeting, and learning what occurs on a day to day basis.

- The HR mentee will research careers in HR and prepare an overview of their findings for the HR mentor for further discussion.

- The HR mentor will invite the HR mentee to an HR leadership meeting where the HR mentor will be presenting HR metrics and updates on HR to the leadership team.

Step 6: Good follow-up throughout the mentoring partnership

- Follow-up meetings to determine progress will be scheduled every two weeks.

- Ongoing communication in between meetings by stopping by HR mentee's work area from time to time to check in. They may also meet up a few times for lunch since they work in the same office.

Step 7: Solid wrap up of the mentoring partnership

- At the end of the ten week mark, they will wrap up with a final meeting.

- The HR mentor will provide the HR mentee with a thank-you/motivational card for all of the accomplishments made during the HR mentoring partnership. They will also invite HR mentee to participate in a task force that will be working on leave of absence administration.

- The HR mentor will also present two books to the HR mentee, one on leaves of absences, and the other covering HR careers.

Step 8: Obtain feedback

- The HR mentor will ask for feedback during the last meeting, and will follow-up with a simple email containing a few additional questions.

Step 9: Follow-up after the mentoring has ended

- The HR mentor and mentee agree to meet for lunch once a month over the next few months to check in.

What I like about this first example is all the potential for growth and personal development for this HR mentee. All of the goals and projects directly link to the HR mentee's own goals and objectives. When I compare where the HR mentee would be prior to the HR mentoring partnership and after the HR mentoring partnership, all I can think of is what a tremendous value this would bring the HR mentee.

I also think about how this HR mentee would feel months down the road if this HR mentoring experience hadn't occurred at all. Would the HR mentee feel more motivated and engaged with or without the HR mentoring experience?

How many others are in a similar place in HR and could benefit from an HR mentoring experience like this?

Example 2: The HR Student

HR Mentee: a student in HR who attended a seminar about HR careers that was presented during a career event at school

HR Mentor: an HR professional who was the presenter at the HR career event

Purpose for HR Mentoring:

In this example, the HR mentee introduced themselves to the speaker and requested mentoring to learn more about careers in HR. The mentee is studying business and human resource management, and has a strong interest in HR careers after graduation. The mentor is very interested in working with HR mentee.

Step 1: Create an impactful first impression

- The HR mentor appreciates the HR mentee's initiative in introducing themselves and requesting

HR mentoring. The HR mentor will start creating an impactful first impression by acknowledging the HR mentee's initiative in an email, along with a request for a day and time for a very brief phone call about the HR mentoring partnership.

- During the phone call, the HR mentor will take the opportunity to share enthusiasm for working with the HR mentee, explain what to expect regarding the process, and explain that an introductory email will be coming which will provide some next steps.

- After the call, the HR mentor will send the introductory email that includes some resources on HR careers that the HR mentee can view right away. Also included in the email is a request to send a copy of their resume, complete a small questionnaire, and to provide a day and time available for the follow-up discussion about the HR mentoring partnership which will be over the phone.

- The mentor will follow-up with a thank-you email for receipt of the resume, the questionnaire, and their availability for next meeting. HR mentor will also send a sample of the meeting agenda for review and feedback from the HR mentee, a confirmation of meeting time, a copy of their own resume, and questionnaire responses for review by the HR mentee.

- The HR mentor will continue making an impactful impression and send the HR mentee a small gift in the mail to help kick off the process, which will be a twenty-four ounce protein shaker with an inspirational HR quote on it and a card.

- During the meeting over the phone, both the HR mentor and mentee will discuss HR courses taken so far, currently taking, and will take prior to graduation. They will discuss other HR interests for the present and for after graduation, determine the desired frequency of meetings going forward, and HR goals and projects. This will all be finalized in an HR Mentoring Agreement.

Step 2: Build an intriguing foundation

- The tools used for building an intriguing foundation for this partnership will be the resume review, questionnaire, and HR Mentoring Agreement.

Step 3: Communicate expectations and roles

- The tools used for communicating expectations for this partnership will be the HR Mentoring Agreement, and ongoing communication during follow-up meetings and in between meetings.

Step 4: Set goals for HR mentoring success

- Meeting Goal: To meet eight times over the phone over the next four months, meeting twice a month.

- HR Goal: To be successful in current HR curriculum. To learn more about HR careers and how to get started. To develop a career plan in HR for after graduation.

- HR Activity Goal: Discuss current coursework and determine areas the HR mentee would like more real life exposure to. Volunteer/intern in an HR department. Meet for an in-person meeting with two HR professional to learn more about their roles.

Step 5: Implement robust HR projects

- The HR mentee will research current entry-level HR positions and prepare an overview for the HR mentor of what would be needed as far as background, skills, and experience to be ready to apply for similar opportunities in the future.

- The HR mentee will volunteer in the alumni career center and observe two on-site job interviews. They will report on their experience to HR mentor.

- The HR mentee will attend an actual employee benefits enrollment meeting at their school and observe the HR team's presentation. They will report their experience and observations to the HR mentor.

- The HR mentee will meet with a Vice President of Human Resources and a Director of Human Resources and report these meeting experiences to the HR mentor.

Step 6: Good follow-up throughout the mentoring partnership

- Follow-up meetings will be scheduled to determine progress twice a month.

- There will be ongoing communication in between meetings via text and email.

Step 7: Solid wrap up of the mentoring partnership

- At the end of the four month mark, the HR mentor and mentee will wrap up with a final meeting.

- The HR mentor will provide the HR mentee with a thank-you/motivational card for all of the accomplishments made during the HR mentoring partnership.

- The HR mentor will also present a resource to the HR mentee on HR careers.

- The HR mentor and mentee agree to a few follow-up activities to occur after the mentoring partnership has ended.

Step 8: Obtain feedback

- The HR mentor will ask for feedback during the last meeting and will follow up with a survey link for HR mentee to complete.

Step 9: Follow-up after the mentoring has ended

- The HR mentor and mentee agree to two follow-up calls; one after thirty days and one after three months.

What I like about this example, is all the benefits of mentoring this HR mentee will receive as a result of stepping out of their comfort zone and reaching out to the HR professional. After the mentoring experience has been completed, this mentee will have exposure to HR activities they may not have had otherwise.

This can certainly help shape the HR mentee's outlook on HR overall, as well as the HR career direction they may choose to pursue as a result of the mentoring experience.

Examples of Other HR Mentoring Formats

While the two examples described represent forms of mentoring in HR, I want to express that there are unlimited ways to use this process to successfully mentor other HR professionals. The following are a few other examples:

Email Mentoring in HR

If you are an HR professional who already has a social media presence in HR, or have access to HR professionals by some other means, then you can consider email mentoring in HR.

This is where you can invite HR professionals to ask you questions about HR and their HR career path. They would have the option to accept your email or online invitation, and gain access to a series of emails that you would send with tips, advice, and suggestions.

Your first email would be the first impression email to welcome them to your process. This email could also include links to free resources that would add to their first impression experience with you. You could also create a free HR report, e-book, or checklist that would be available for each HR mentee to access.

There are so many ways this format can grow as the interest in working with you as an HR mentor grows. You could create your own HR mentoring website or blog, and even use an email service where you can create an email series, newsletters, or any other communication that would be sent to your HR mentee's email inbox automatically after they accept your invitation.

Even though this is a mentoring process through email, you can still have as much interaction as you wish with your HR mentees by recommending HR goals and projects for them to achieve, offering periodic live webinars for them to join, and so much more. You would do this all while requesting their feedback and input along the way.

Email mentoring in HR is a great option to share your HR expertise to as many HR professionals that you can reach in this format.

Group Mentoring in HR

Group mentoring in HR can take many forms. For example, you may have a group of HR professionals who would be mentored by one HR mentor. Or you could have a group of

HR mentors who would all work with a group of HR professionals.

There are so many ways to use group mentoring in HR that work effectively and are a lot of fun. By getting the groups together, throughout the mentoring process, allows for mentors and mentees to also learn from each other.

Roundtable Mentoring in HR

This style of mentoring in HR would allow for a group of HR mentee's to have access to several HR professionals, each in different areas of HR. This would allow for an opportunity to learn about each individual HR professional's typical day, job and challenges in HR in their respective HR specialty.

You could simply have a group of HR professionals together on a stage/table and share their own background and experiences. Then allow time for the group of HR mentee's to ask questions of them individually or as a group.

Quick Mentoring in HR

This approach to mentoring in HR would be great for an event that is a quick, one-time event. For example, you could have a one-day event where HR professionals are available for a short period of time. During this time, HR mentees would be partnered with an HR professional for questions, discussion, and advice in areas of HR.

You could also add a component where they can meet with several HR professionals during this time. For example, they could get 15-30 min with one HR professional, then at the designated time switch to a new HR professional for another round of conversation. This could continue for 3-4 rounds and they would have had exposure to several one-on-one conversations with several different HR professionals during a single event.

Reverse Mentoring in HR

This style of mentoring in HR would allow for an HR mentor to learn from the HR mentee. This role reversal in the HR mentoring process can be very beneficial to help learn specific information from the HR mentee's perspective.

Peer Mentoring in HR

This approach to mentoring in HR would allow for HR peers to get involved in the mentoring process. For example, you may have one HR person who could mentor someone on their same team or similar position.

This would be a great development opportunity for that individual to mentor someone else. They could mentor someone new to the team, or in HR, and contribute to their successful transition.

Other Mentoring in HR Options

In addition to all of the examples I have provided on how you can approach mentoring in HR, there still may be other ideas that you have on how you would like to implement an HR mentoring process in your own unique way.

There are so many possibilities that exist on how you can accomplish this and I am hopeful that the ideas that have been discussed in this book will truly help you get started.

You may decide that you want to try several approaches to get a better idea of what works best for you. Or you may decide that incorporating more than one format into your process is exactly what you would like to do. You may even have other ideas that are not included in this book on how you would like your mentoring in HR process to look like.

Whatever approach you decide, just know that this is a flexible process that you can adjust or enhance at any time.

| **Watch Video Message: Alisa Charles on Chapter 5** https:///hrinventurenetwork.com/alisa-charles-chapter5 | |

6 | *My Final Thoughts on Mentoring in HR*

I am hopeful that you have reviewed the examples of how you can utilize the 9 steps to successful mentoring in HR. You should now have a better idea of how you can implement this process into a program you create.

The following are a few final thoughts I have on mentoring in HR:

Make this Process Your Own

The key is to create a process that incorporates your own vision and unique style. By creating a system that reflects your ideal mentoring situation, it will increase your enthusiasm toward the process which will benefit the HR mentee.

This is my desire for you and for any other HR professional who may be looking to share their HR expertise to help others in HR too.

Recognition

Keep in mind that successful mentoring in HR can be used as a tool to recognize members of your HR team. For those HR professionals in your HR world who are looking for opportunities to grow and develop, you can create a system that will help them mentor others in HR.

Additionally, you may know of others who could benefit from being mentored, such as HR students or other members of your HR team who you work with. You can create a program where those individuals can be invited to be mentored. That could be a way to recognize their efforts by offering them dedicated time to work with an HR mentor to help them achieve certain goals.

Recruitment Strategy

Creating successful mentoring in HR experiences for others in HR can become a great recruitment source for future opportunities. Imagine having a group of HR mentees who you can reach out to about open HR positions? You may be able to consider them for open positions, or they may be able to refer you to someone they know. This could certainly be one strategy that can be incorporated into an overall recruitment plan for future HR openings.

Mentoring Beyond HR

Another avenue for the successful mentoring in HR process is that it doesn't have to be used solely in HR. You can use the tools and resource in this book to create a system that includes multiple areas outside of HR.

This can be achieved by simply replacing any HR-specific items with more general items, or even other department (non-HR) specific items. Creating a mentoring program across multiple functional areas can benefit many employees.

This could be an opportunity for you to create a mentoring process that you can introduce in your organization. It may also result in even greater exposure in your HR career, with a process that could positively impact many other employees in your workplace.

This could be a great way to move beyond your own comfort zone as an HR professional and try something new in HR.

Where to find HR mentees?

There are several ways to find individuals within HR who may be interested in being mentored.

Company/Department:

Check within your own department or organization to find potential HR mentees. If you work for a large organization, there may already be a large pool of HR professionals who are early in their careers who may be interested in being mentored. You might have individuals right where you are who are new to the HR world and could benefit from being mentored.

College/University:

Another way to find potential HR mentees could be to partner with a college or university that has an HR program. Often times there might be opportunities to collaborate with an HR program that would love the opportunity for their students to partner with an HR professional.

You could also check with your local HR association, where they may already have a partnership with a college or university where you might have an opportunity to mentor HR students.

People You Know:

There may be individuals you know or who know of others who may be interested in being mentored in HR. This could be people inside your HR world or outside of work who may know of such individuals.

You could also ask them if they are aware of others who may be looking for mentoring who they can refer you to.

Individuals Who Reach Out to You:

There may be times where individuals may have reached out to you on social media, at an event, or in other ways, and expressed an interest in wanting to learn more about HR. You could certainly choose to make yourself available as an HR mentor and help those individuals who actually reach out to you.

I am hopeful that these final thoughts on mentoring in HR has provided even greater ideas on how you can make this process work for you. Since there has been a lot of information shared with you, I would like to provide 10 reminders to think about as you consider putting your own unique process together.

The following are 10 reminders about successful mentoring in HR to think about when getting started with creating a process of your own.

Watch Video Message: Alisa Charles on Chapter 6 https:///hrinventurenetwork.com/alisa-charles-chapter6	

7 | 10 Things to Remember About Successful Mentoring in HR

1. Remember your reasons for your interest in mentoring other HR professionals

One of the first things I recommend that you remember about mentoring in HR, is your purpose and interest in mentoring in HR. This sets a good foundation by reminding you of what excites you about helping others in HR. It will also be the motivation that can help you overcome obstacles that may arise throughout the journey.

We've discussed at length about all the different reasons why someone might want to mentor in HR. Once you remember your reason for mentoring, it will help you in those moments where you may start to think about stopping the journey, or feeling like you don't have enough time for mentoring others. By going back and remembering the reasons why you were interested in doing this initially, it should help motivate and inspire you to keep moving forward.

Your desire to want to help others in HR is important. It may be that there is someone out there who could really use your help in the unique style that only you can offer.

Take another look at your purpose for mentoring and why you want to do it. Then really build on that as your foundation to create an awesome process that any HR professional or student would be able to benefit from by working with you and learning from all your experiences in HR.

I am sure you have spent a lot of time building your career. I am also pretty sure you have had many ups and downs in your career, and your experiences can help someone else. You may be able to help someone avoid some of the pitfalls you may have experienced. Or maybe someone is going through something right now and a few encouraging words from you could make all the difference in how they approach real life HR situations.

I want to encourage you to remember why you are interested in mentoring in HR, and to use that as your starting point to create an awesome mentoring in HR experience.

2. Commit to taking one step at a time once you have decided to mentor

Once you have your mind set on mentoring in HR, you may be tempted to pull all the steps together all at once, which can be overwhelming. Instead, just take one step at a time and you will begin to see your own unique process come to life.

Be sure to take your time to get the results that you want. Whether it's a formal process or an informal one, it will become the process that works best for you. Enjoy the journey.

3. Be confident in your ability to positively impact another HR professional

You have spent a lot of time building your HR career, and as a result, you have a lot to offer another HR professional or a student. There are individuals out there who would really appreciate your support, knowledge, and the opportunity to learn from you.

If you have any concerns about what you can offer to another individual who is interested in HR, then one recommendation I have for you is to write down all the things you have done in HR. I would suggest you start with the first ten things you can think of that you have accomplished as your starting point.

You can then refer to your resume, and remind yourself of all of the amazing things you have accomplished in HR that might be able to help someone.

4. Be proactive in how to manage your time to fit in mentoring

As HR professionals, there are so many priorities that we juggle at work each day. This could create some hesitancy about mentoring due to feeling like there just isn't enough time.

By having a plan to manage your time, it will give you the opportunity to get out of your normal routine and try something different.

To find more time to fit mentoring into your schedule, decide what things you can delegate, what things you can put on hold for later, and what things you can stop doing.

By rearranging some of your other priorities, you may find just the time you need for mentoring in HR.

5. Research how mentoring in HR can help you receive recertification credit

In addition to giving back to someone else in HR when you decide to mentor, it may also be an opportunity for you to receive recertification credit if you are a certified HR professional.

Why not receive credit for your contribution to the field of HR, by researching how you could structure mentoring in such a way to earn recertification credit?

Obtaining an HR certification is a huge accomplishment, and the only way to maintain your certification is to keep up with your recertification credits. Be sure to research all the information needed to receive recertification credit. Then create a process that will help you with meeting the requirements to receive credit.

6. Be prepared to make this a two-way street

In addition to giving great advice and sharing your experiences in HR, I also want to encourage you to use the mentoring experience as a learning opportunity for yourself as well. It's a great way to find out what students are learning in their HR curriculum, and to expand your knowledge regarding processes that occur in other departments and/or other companies.

Don't go into this feeling like you have to make all the contributions. Instead, it should be a shared experience where both are contributing and learning from the HR mentoring partnership.

7. Maximize the opportunity to enhance your own HR career

Another thing to think about when it comes to mentoring in HR, are ways to enhance your own HR career. I have talked a lot about how to have a greater sense of purpose in the things we do in our careers and in our lives. What better way to enhance your own career than by either mentoring someone, or giving back in some other way?

We all have a purpose or something we were meant to accomplish. When operating outside of that purpose, we can feel a lot of frustration, or that we are not making a difference.

Ensure that you use this as an opportunity to determine how this experience can enhance your own HR career by doing something different in HR.

8. Create a system that will work for you

I am very excited about all the opportunities that exist in mentoring others in HR. This is your opportunity to create a system that works especially for you.

For example, if you know that you can only do mentoring over the phone, that's fine. That works great when the mentor and mentee are in different location from each other. If the opportunity exists to be able to meet your HR mentee in person, that works too. Whatever makes sense for you to incorporate into your own process is the system that is right for you as an HR mentor.

You can also determine if you want to make this a short-term or a long-term assignment, as well as how many people you might want to mentor at a time. You may want to mentor someone new every quarter or every year. You can customize a process that meets your personal aspirations and the vision you have for mentoring others in HR.

9. Share the idea of mentoring with other HR professionals

Once you have made the decision to mentor others in HR, you may want to share this idea with other HR professionals who may also be interested in doing something similar.

You may all decide to do this together, with the goal of giving back to other HR professionals and students. You can share this with other HR professionals in your department or others you know outside of your organization who might be interested.

Inspiring others to help HR professionals and students is a great way to motivate those around you to do something different in HR. There's a good chance that you are surrounded by like-minded individuals who have also built their HR career and would like to share their knowledge, skills, and expertise with others as well.

10. Be determined to make this an awesome mentoring experience

There's been a lot of discussion about mentoring others in HR up to this point. We've discussed processes, tools, resources, approaches, and everything in between. My hope for you in reading this book is not just to discuss the basics of developing a process that you can use to mentor others in HR. I also hope that you will truly make it an incredible experience for another HR professional - one that will impact them for the rest of their career.

Don't get too caught up in a perfect process right at the start, or feeling like you have to use every single tool all at once. You can gradually introduce different pieces of this as it makes sense to do so. For example, your great HR mentoring experience may start off as a very informal process. Then as you move along, you may want to introduce an assessment, or put together a job description, or introduce some of the other tools that make this more of a customized process for you.

This book was designed to simply give you some ideas to get you started. However, I don't want you to ever lose sight of the purpose of mentoring others in HR. It is to positively impact others in HR with a mentoring experience they can carry with them as they move forward in their HR careers and in life.

How amazing would it be if one day down the road, your HR mentee reflects on their mentoring experience with you and shares how much you've impacted them? It would be an amazing thing for someone to share how much you've made a difference.

Your Next Steps

We have now come to the part where it's time for action. Are you ready to make a plan to start creating your own successful mentoring in HR process?

I want to encourage you to simply take it one step at a time. Review each step and determine what you would like that step to look like for your own unique process.

Remember, this is the exciting part! This is where you now have lots of information that will help you form a process that can positively impact the HR careers for others in HR and beyond.

I am so excited to see where successful mentoring in HR will take you. Feel free to keep me posted on your journey with an email to alisa@hrinventurenetwork.com at any time.

The following is a checklist to help you with your next steps:

Checklist

- ✓ Identify your purpose and goals for becoming an HR mentor
- ✓ Determine who your ideal HR mentee would be
- ✓ Research in advance criteria required for mentoring in HR to qualify for recertification credit
- ✓ Determine method for initial communication to welcome new HR mentee (phone call/email/in person)
- ✓ Identify any relevant tools and resources you may want to have available to provide to HR mentee (company brochures, HR tools and tips, information on upcoming HR meetings in the area, helpful links)
- ✓ Determine how roles and expectations will be established and communicated
- ✓ Consider developing an HR Mentoring Agreement that can be used to confirm the details of the mentoring partnership in writing

- ✓ Determine what HR goals, projects, or activities will be part of process
- ✓ Determine frequency of meetings and length of partnership
- ✓ Confirm your plan on how you will follow-up with mentee during the mentoring arrangement
- ✓ Develop a positive exit process
- ✓ Determine how you will acknowledge accomplishments and successes in a meaningful way
- ✓ Develop list of wrap up activities
- ✓ Determine how you will obtain feedback on the process
- ✓ Determine what follow-up you will do after the mentoring has ended

Conclusion

In conclusion, I would like to thank you again for your interest in successful mentoring in HR and for reading this book. I want to encourage you to read these steps as many times as you wish, and to create a process that will help you make a difference in HR. You can make an impact in an unique way, based on your own gifts, talents, and experiences. The time is now and I am hopeful that you will begin taking action today.

Other Resources

Learn how you can take mentoring in HR to the next level with fifteen complimentary *Mentoring in HR* templates by using the link below. Wishing you much success in your mentoring in HR journey.

http://www.hrinventurenetwork.com/get-15-free-templates/

alisa@hrinventurenetwork.com

Watch Video Message: Alisa Charles on Chapter 7 https:///hrinventurenetwork.com/wishing-you-success-in-mentoring-in-hr	

If you liked this book, then you may be interested in the following journal for HR professionals also by Alisa Charles.

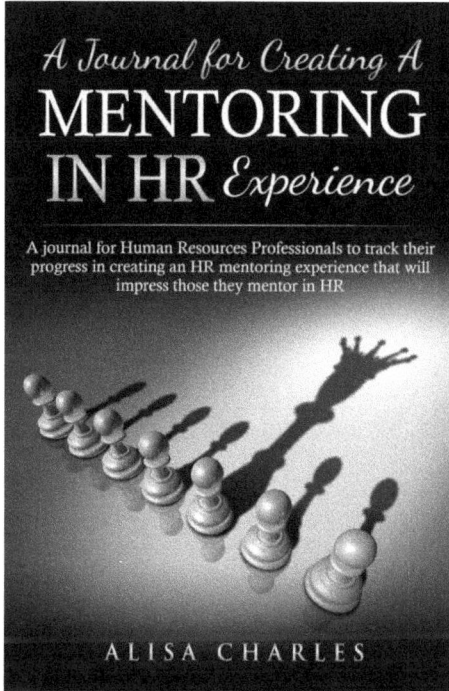

A Journal for Creating A Mentoring in HR Experience

A journal for Human Resources Professionals to track their progress in creating an HR mentoring experience that will impress those they mentor in HR

www.hrinventurenetwork.com/journals4hr

www.ingramcontent.com/pod-product-compliance
Lightning Source LLC
Chambersburg PA
CBHW060618210326
41520CB00010B/1391